The Secret

by Julie Haydon

illustrated by Kiera Poelsma

Last Saturday morning,
Tess and her mum were walking
past Alex's house.
They saw Alex's mum at her car.

"Hi," said Tess.

3

Alex's mum jumped.

"I didn't see you there, Tess," she said.

"Alex isn't home.
He's out with his dad."

Tess saw a shiny red bike
in the back of the car.
"Is that bike for Alex's birthday?"
she asked.

"Yes," said Alex's mum.

"But it's a secret, Tess. You can't tell Alex."

"I won't tell Alex," said Tess.
"I can keep a secret."

All week, Alex talked about his birthday.

Tess wanted to tell him about the shiny red bike. But it was a secret!

The next Saturday,
Alex had a birthday
party at his house.

He raced up to Tess.
"Come and look at
what I got!" he said.

13

Alex showed off his new bike.

Alex's mum came and stood next to Tess. "Thanks for keeping the secret, Tess," she said.

Tess smiled.

"I *can* keep a secret."